Up to You, Porky

Victoria Wood

UP TO YOU, PORKY
The Victoria Wood Sketch Book

METHUEN

by the same author

Lucky Bag: The Victoria Wood Song Book

First published in Great Britain in 1985
by Methuen London Ltd
11 New Fetter Lane, London EC4P 4EE
Reprinted 1986
Copyright © Victoria Wood 1985
Made and printed in Great Britain by
Hazell Watson & Viney Limited,
Member of the BPCC Group,
Aylesbury, Bucks

BRITISH LIBRARY CATALOGUING IN PUBLICATION DATA

Wood, Victoria
  Up to you, Porky: the Victoria Wood sketch book.
  I. Title
  828'.91409   PN175

ISBN 0-413-59930-2

To Peter Eckersley, who liked a laugh

Contents

List of Illustrations

THIGS I LIKE

by Vicky Wood age 32

The thigs I like are dferent ones. One is wen I am wasing
pulester trosers in my wahing maschine and I rember not to
open the door wen it is in PAUS and full of water and the water
do not go on me.

ANothe thig I like is wen I have ben shovling anthercite and
I sneze and it coms all black on my sleave then I know my nose
hares are woking propaly.

A thiNg I like allso is wen I am cleanig my Hondaccord befor
a jurnyllist has to to get in ti it and I Find a very small
peice of FrutAnD nut I eat it under the grealever. A thin
I do not like is wen I find FuitandNUT under wehre my bottom
gos and it is meltied on to the vellor veloo fuzzy stuff.

Anothe thign I like is wen pople come up to me and dig me in
the papershop and sey Pleases settle a bet I stand to lose a
gin and pep on this?ar you or ar yuo not Jiulie Walters and
I say no and they look ded dispointed but I do not care and
think ha-ha-ha like MUTTLEY in WACKY RACES

And I like as well wen the man from MEPHTHUN(cant spell it)pone up
and say we have some lambnatid covers gong begging do yuo have
any old skechs we will pay hansomly but not for ages.
And the last thig I like is wen I haev filled a hwole page
and i can stop writing and watsh WACKY RACES.

So that is the end of THIGS I LKE

Skin Care

*A department store. An over-made-up sales assistant is
behind the cosmetics counter. A girl enters.*

Assistant	Good morning, madam. May I interest you in our skin-care range, though I have to admit that from here your skin looks flawless?
Girl	Thank you.
Assistant	But then again, I failed my driving test because I couldn't read the number plate. *Do* you have any spots?
Girl	No.
Assistant	Would you like some? I'll just do a quick check on the computer. Colour of eyes?
Girl	Blue.
Assistant	Grey. Hair?
Girl	Blonde.
Assistant	Mousey. Condition of pores: open, closed?
Girl	They're sort of ajar.
Assistant	Let's see. Dear me. To we in the trade, that's not so much of a complexion – more of a doily.
Girl	Don't you sell a product that would close them up a bit?
Assistant	Well, we do an astringent, but really, with pores that big, you'd be better off with a darning needle and some pink wool. You see, it's really your greasy skin that's at fault.
Girl	Is it?
Assistant	We do sell this – I don't know if it's strong enough for what you need, but it brought my chip-pan up lovely.
Girl	I'm starting to feel quite bad about what I look like.
Assistant	Good. Now, about your wrinkles.
Girl	Laughter lines.
Assistant	Nothing's that funny. We can arrange plastic surgery. £15 including bed and breakfast.
Girl	Why is it so cheap?
Assistant	The surgeon's bleeding hopeless.

Girl	Well, it sounds like I'm so ugly, nothing's going to be any use.
Assistant	Oh, I don't know, madam. There's our special formula lipstick.
Girl	What good's that?
Assistant	It's six foot high, you can stand behind it. Can I help you madam?

Brontëburgers

Guide   Right, I'm your official guide. Now before I show you round, I'll just fill you in on a few details, as we call them. As you can see, we're standing in the hall of the Haworth Parsonage, where Haworth's parson, the Reverend Brontë, lived here with his daughters, the famous Brontë sisters, now, alas, no longer with us – but they have left us their novels, which I've not read, being more of a Dick Francis nut. Now, if you pass by me into the parlour (mind my vaccination) ... This is what was known in those days as a parlour, somewhat similar to our lounge-type sitting-room affair in modern terminology. I'm afraid the wallpaper isn't the original period to which we're referring to, it is actually Laura Ashley, but I think it does give some idea of what life must have been like in a blustery old Yorkshire community of long ago.

That portrait on the wall is actually of Charlotte Brontë, one of the famous Brontë sisters, and of course to us she may seem a rather gloomy-looking individual; but you must remember these days she'd have a perm, or blusher, or I suppose even drugs would have helped her maintain a more cheerful attitude. In fact, she'd probably not be dead if she was alive today. Now if you'd like to hutch through to the Reverend Brontë's study ... This is a typical study in which to do studying – as you can see there's a table, chair ... (oh my poncho, I've been looking for that ...) and I like to imagine this elderly old gentleman hunched over a sermon, probably thinking, 'Where's my cocoa, I suppose those darn girls are in the middle of another chapter,' or something like that he may have been thinking – we just can't be sure ... Of course he died eventually, unfortunately. You must remember this is an extremely exposed part of the United Kingdom, I mean, it's May now, and I'm still having to slip that polo-neck under my bolero.

On the table we see the Reverend Brontë's gloves. They tell us such a lot about him. He had two hands, and he wasn't missing any fingers. We think they were knitted by one of the famous Brontë sisters. I don't suppose their brother Branwell could knit and anyway being an alcoholic he'd never have been able to cast on.

Now if you'd just hutch up the stairs ... We're looking out over the graves to the hills beyond. And, fairly clearly in the distance we can hear the wind 'wuthering'. That's an old Yorkshire word; some other old Yorkshire words are 'parkin' and 'fettle'. The room in which we're now standing in was originally Charlotte's mother's bedroom. In fact Charlotte's mother died in this room, and Charlotte died in here too, so better not stay too long! (Just my joke!) In that glass case you'll see what we call a day dress – that is a dress worn in the day, not at night – we think belonging to Anne or Emily, presumably not Branwell, unless he had more problems than history's prepared to tell us.

A few dates for the date-minded. The Brontë family moved here some time in the nineteenth century, and lived here for quite a number of years. As I say, Charlotte died in this room – those are her slippers. And I like to imagine her in this room, with her slippers on, dying.

Now if you go through the far door, yes, do move my moped ... Now this room was at one time Branwell's room. I think people tend to forget Branwell was fairly artistic himself. Of course, he was lazy, conceited and a dipsomaniac, so these days he'd have probably been in the government.

Now if anybody would like a souvenir to take home as a souvenir, we have Brontë video-games, body-warmers, acrylic mitts, pedestal mats, feminine deodorants and novelty tea-strainers. Snacks and light refreshments are available in the Heathcliff Nosher Bar, so please feel free to sample our very popular Brontëburgers. Or for the fibre-conscious – our Branwell Brontëburgers.

Oh – just a little message for the 'Yorkshire Heritage' coach party. Can they please re-convene at two in the car-park ready for this afternoon's trip which is, I believe, round three dark Satanic mills, Emmerdale Farm, and Nora Batty's front room? Thank you.

The Woman with 740 Children

A battered-looking housewife opens the door to a bright young reporter.

Reporter   *(in doorway)* Mrs Mather? Kate Harnson – *Weekly Woman.*
Woman   Oh yes, come in. *(The reporter takes her coat off in hall.)*
You'll have to excuse the mess.
Reporter   Good heavens, it's not surprising. Is it true you had the
biggest surviving multiple birth in the world?
Woman   I believe that's correct, yes. Anyway – come through.

*They go into a room absolutely packed with little children,
toddlers and babies. Also dummy babies lying on floor, on
mantelpiece, top of TV etc. The reporter looks round for
somewhere to sit down. All the chairs are covered in babies.*

Sit down – just put them on the floor.
Reporter   *(opening her notebook)* I'll just get the details first. How
many babies did you actually have?
Woman   We think it was seven hundred and forty-two, but a couple
got mislaid when we left the hospital – about seven
hundred and forty we think now.
Reporter   And this was all as a result of taking a new fertility drug?
Woman   Well not exactly. We'd been married twelve years and I
hadn't, you know, conceived. I blamed it on my husband
because he'd had an accident leap-frogging over a drinking
fountain. But anyway, the doctors said no way could I have
babies until we consummated the marriage – well by that
time I was desperate – I'd tried everything else. So – I
won't dwell on the ins and outs but we had two marvellous
doctors and they talked us through the whole thing.
Reporter   What about the fertility drug?

Woman	I took that off my own bat. It came free with a magazine. It wasn't your one it was the other woman's one. I took a double dose because my sister only has it for the serial, and that and the sex – that's the medical term – did the trick.
Reporter	I suppose it was a tremendous shock?
Woman	Well yes, I was hoping to give birth to a seven-year-old girl, but …
Reporter	Must have been a tremendously long labour.
Woman	Well, the doctor that delivered the first one, he's retired now. I know by the time it was all over the pound was only worth seventy-five pence.
Reporter	I suppose your day is one long round of feeding and changing?
Woman	Not really. I never eat breakfast and I keep the same clothes on all day.
Reporter	I meant the babies. I should have thought just feeding them was a full-time job?
Woman	Well it would be if I gave in to them. I mean when I first came home from the hospital it was four-hourly bottles and sterilising everything – after two days I'd had enough. I dragged them all into the kitchen, I said here's the grill, there's the fish-fingers, get on with it.
Reporter	Didn't they complain?
Woman	Well most of them can't talk yet thank goodness. I got a few dirty looks obviously.
Reporter	You seem to have things pretty well under control now – what problems do you anticipate as they get older?
Woman	Just when they go to school and I have to listen to the same knock-knock joke seven hundred and forty times, having to hide seven hundred and forty selection boxes on top of the wardrobe, that kind of thing …
Reporter	Has your husband been helpful?
Woman	Very. He left me.
Reporter	And other people?
Woman	Incredibly kind. They send clothes – they're not baby clothes but the thought's there.
Reporter	Has there been any talk of sponsorship?
Woman	One television company has shown great interest in one of the children, thinks he has great potential.
Reporter	Oh really? Which one?

Woman	Now you're asking. No idea. All look the same to me *(lifting one out from under a cushion).* They get everywhere.
Reporter	Well thank you very much for taking time off to talk to me.
Woman	Not at all. Here, would you like a couple to take home with you?
Reporter	No, really –
Woman	No bother. We've got loads. I'll just find you a carrier. *(She comes back with two babies in a box.)* OK? Can you see yourself out? *(The reporter leaves.)* All right – I wasn't going to embarrass you in front of company, but which one of you's nicked my fags?

Girls Talking

Film. A street. Jeanette and Marie in school uniform (ankle socks, track shoes, short skirts, shirts and ties etc) leaning against the wall. A male interviewer is heard in voice over throughout the film.

Interviewer Jeanette is fifteen, Marie is fourteen and a half. Both are from broken homes and living in an area with a high level of unemployment.

Jeanette Not really been to school since I was five. Five or six. I go in, like, if there's something happening, like vaccination, or a nativity play.

Cut to Marie in mid-speech.

Marie Well it's just boring like, isn't it? They don't teach you about anything important – like how to inject yourself, it's all geography and things.

Interviewer Maybe you think it's not worth being qualified as there are so few jobs in Liverpool ... ?

Jeanette There is lots of jobs. The government wants to keep us unemployed so we won't smoke on the buses.

Cut to Jeanette.

I could have been in a film but it was boring ...

Interviewer What film was that?

Jeanette Documentary on child prostitution.

Interviewer You've actually been a prostitute?

Jeanette Yeah but it was boring. The sex was all right but they kept wanting you to talk to them.

Cut to Marie.

Marie Music? Kid's stuff really, isn't it?

Jeanette	The government puts things on the record underneath the music.
Interviewer	Sorry?
Jeanette	Like, you know, messages that you can only hear with your brain.
Interviewer	What do they say?
Jeanette	Like telling you what to do.
Marie	Keep you under.
Jeanette	Don't say 'tits' in the reference library.
Marie	Don't gob on each other.
Interviewer	Is there much sleeping around amongst young people?
Marie	No, it's boring.
Jeanette	It's like for your Mums and Dads really, isn't it?
Marie	Like drinking.
Interviewer	Don't you and your, er, mates drink?
Jeanette	We used to drink battery acid.
Marie	But it burns holes in your tights.
Interviewer	Do you sniff glue?
Jeanette	That's for snobs really, isn't it?
Marie	Grammar school kids sniff glue.
Jeanette	We sniff burning lino.
Marie	Cot blankets.
Jeanette	Estée Lauder Youth Dew.
Interviewer	What effect does it have?
Marie	Fall over mainly.
Interviewer	Doesn't sniffing heighten your emotions?
Jeanette	Oh yeah, you get a lot more bored.
Marie	Things that were a bit boring get really boring, and that's great.
Interviewer	How do you see your future – do you think you'll get married?
Jeanette	We'd like to, 'cos it's easier to get Valium if you're married.
Marie	But we can't can we?
Interviewer	Why?
Jeanette	The government are bringing out this thing – you can't get married unless you've got a going-away outfit. It's got to be –
Marie	Suit.
Jeanette	Yeah, suit, and it's got to be in two colours that match.

Marie	And you have to have a handbag and slingbacks.
Jeanette	It's just not on.
Marie	My mother's got enough to do paying off my shoplifting fine.
Interviewer	What happened?
Jeanette	A duvet fell into my shopping bag.

Cut.

Interviewer	Have either of you got boyfriends?
Jeanette	We have, like, one between two.
Marie	Just to save time really.
Interviewer	And what does your boyfriend do?
Marie	He gets tattooed a lot.
Interviewer	Yes, what else does he do?
Jeanette	He has them removed a lot.

Cut.

Interviewer	Any ambitions?
Jeanette	I'd like some stretch denims.
Interviewer	I suppose you can't afford any?
Jeanette	You can apply for a grant.
Marie	For denims.
Jeanette	But not stretch denims.
Interviewer	How do you feel about teenage pregnancies?
Marie	We've got used to them now.

They sniff a bottle of perfume. Jeanette falls over. Marie looks bored.

Young Love: One

Carl and Gail are a slow-witted Northern pair, sitting on a wall because they can't think of anywhere to go.

Gail Do you love me, Carl?
Carl Yeah, you're all right.
Gail Do you think about me when you're cleaning windows?
Carl Yeah, some of the time.
Gail Do you think about me when you're having your dinner?
Carl Depends what it is.
Gail What do you mean, Carl?
Carl I might if I'm having a Scotch egg, but if I'm having crisps, I'm concentrating on opening t' bag, aren't I?
Gail What about at night?
Carl What about at night?
Gail Do you think about me then?
Carl In bed?
Gail Yeah, or under it.
Carl When I'm in bed, Gail, I'm reading *The Puzzler*, aren't I?
Gail Yeah, but, when your mam's put light out, and you've just closed your eyes, what do you think about then, Carl?
Carl My shammy leather.

Pause.

Gail When we get married, Carl, where will we live?
Carl Well, we're living in my mam's sideboard, aren't we?
Gail Yeah, but after that. Shall we have an 'ouse?
Carl Nah. Penthouse flat.
Gail What's that, Carl?
Carl It's got fur rugs, hasn't it?
Gail What colour?
Carl Well, it depends, dunnit? If it's off an animal, it'll be animal-coloured, won't it? Or there's orange.

Gail Where is it?

Carl What?

Gail This flat.

Carl Well, they're all in London, aren't they? And there's two in the Isle of Man.

Gail Is that the same as France?

Carl France is abroad i'n't it? They have different bread and allsorts.

Gail Different allsorts? You mean not liquorice?

Carl Eh? Anyway, they're on t'roof.

Gail What?

Carl Penthouse flats.

Gail I'm not living on a roof. My knitting'll roll into t'guttering.

Carl Who's been telling you about guttering?

Gail You did. When we were kissing goodnight last night, and we snuggled up, and you said you had something to tell me, and you told me about guttering.

Carl Yeah, well, I won't always be that romantic.

Gail OK Carl.

This Week's Film

Voice over This week's film is a wartime classic telling of the exploits of the happy-go-lucky crew of a Lancaster bomber. Made in 1941, we bring you *Dropping Them on Dover.*

Jean stands by the window staring out into the night. She waves as the planes go by. There is a knock on the door. Enter Smithy, an RAF chap nervously gripping his cap.

Jean	Hello Smithy. Where's Bob?
Smithy	He isn't with me, Jean.
Jean	Go on.
Smithy	He's bought it.
Jean	I see. I think I knew, you know. I think he knew. As he left yesterday morning he turned at the gate and called, 'Jean, don't save my bloater'. What happened?
Smithy	Are you sure you want to hear? It's not awfully pleasant.
Jean	War never is. Go on.
Smithy	*(sitting down and lighting his pipe)* As you know, we're a pretty ramshackle bunch. The wireless operator can only get *ITMA* and the rear-gunner won't sit with his back to the engine. And I guess the old bomber isn't up to much.
Jean	What do you mean?
Smithy	Well it's not a Lancaster, it's a Silver Cross. There isn't a bay for bombs, just a tray underneath where you put your shopping. Well last night we were over the Moehne Dam.
Jean	But you bombed that last month.
Smithy	Yes, but Bob thought we should go back and see if that's where he'd left his ration book. On the way back the port engine started to misfire.
Mother	But wasn't it checked before you took off?
Smithy	Well yes but – God, the boys are young now. My ground crew do their best but, you know, they've got homework to do ... Cubs ...

Jean	What happened, Smithy?
Smithy	The starboard engine went, we lost height, we were over land but didn't know where.
Jean	Go on.
Smithy	Bob gave the order 'Bail out and if you're caught pretend to be German'.
Jean	That's terrible.
Smithy	Yes it was. Bob landed first – said, 'Heil Hitler' in his best accent and was stabbed to death with a pitchfork.
Jean	Why?
Smithy	We'd landed in Margate.
Jean	Poor Bob. He always was a bit of a duffer.
Smithy	Jean?
Jean	Yes Smithy?
Smithy	It may be too soon to ask you this, but I've always admired you and if I don't ask now I never will.
Jean	Go on Smithy.
Smithy	Could I have his bloater?

Music.

In the Office

Beattie	You look tired, Connie.
Connie	I couldn't get off last night. I even had Dick throw a brick at my head to stun me but …
Beattie	Have you tried jamming your head in the tumble-drier and switching on?
Connie	No?
Beattie	It worked for me. Then of course the body gets accustomed.
Connie	Like deodorants. They work for a certain amount of time and then bang – people are backing away with handbags over their noses.
Beattie	You're not ponging too badly at the minute, Connie.
Connie	I've had my armpits stripped. A peel-off paste. Quite simple to apply though it has marked my cork flooring.
Beattie	Oh, do you have cork? We have tufted shag.
Connie	We have to be able to mop, you see, with Dad's habits …
Beattie	Dicky bladder?
Connie	We call him Dad, but … he can trot to the bogetory as neat as you please when he's not engrossed, but if it's Mavis Nicholson or the Cooking Canon then he won't budge and there you are with it all over your adjustable seating.
Beattie	Can't you put him in a home?
Connie	Well we could, but I'm using his head for a flower arrangement at the moment.
Beattie	Is that an evening class?
Connie	Yes. I put down for Ju Jitsu but I came out of the wrong lift.
Beattie	What's in your sandwiches?
Connie	Soap powder. I think it's these drugs I'm on. Quite nice though. What's yours?
Beattie	Coconut matting. I'm doing the high-fibre.
Connie	Did you watch the news?
Beattie	The nine o'clock?
Connie	Yes. Nasty blouse.

Beattie	We stayed up for *News at Ten*. Three bangles and a polo-neck, thank you.
Connie	No, her ears are in the wrong place for a polo-neck.
Beattie	You need to be Princess Di, really.
Connie	They've the length of bone, haven't they, royalty?
Beattie	The Queen's not got long bones.
Connie	No, well she's spent all that time stood about – with natives waggling their doodahs at her.
Beattie	My cousin's on Male Surgical and she's very short – must be the same thing – the standing.
Connie	Is that the one who went on *Opportunity Knocks* dressed as a cheese and tomato sandwich?
Beattie	No, that was Madge. She didn't win. She got out of rhythm with the xylophone.
Connie	Our next-door's had sex again last night.
Beattie	Not again!
Connie	I mean, I like a joke, but that's twice this month. I could not think what the noise was. I thought our central heating had come on a month early. And then somebody called out, 'Don't bother Ken, I'll do it myself', and I thought, well it can't be the central heating. Have you got gas?
Beattie	No, methane. Well I thought, why not, while I'm on the high-fibre …
Connie	Does it work the cooker as well?
Beattie	Oh yes, though a leg of pork takes seven days to cook through.
Connie	I can't keep it down, pork. Not since a Jehovah's witness told me about their mating habits.
Beattie	Pigs? What do they do? *(She glances off.)*
Connie	They enjoy it.
Beattie	They don't.
Connie	They do. Now, are you still having pork and pickle fancies for Shona's wedding?
Beattie	I'm not.

Phone rings.

Family Planning, can I help you?

Dotty on Women's Lib

Dotty Good evening. Here I am again – in spite of a touch of groin strain. Some of you may be shocked to hear the word, but I believe in getting these things out in the open – I was the first woman in our crescent to say 'boob', and I've never regretted it.

Now, where was I? Oh, yes, my groin. Nothing to worry about – had a heavy day's hoovering yesterday, and I'm afraid I got carried away behind the cistern with my crevice-tool.

Now, the other evening I was snuggled up to Daddy in the lounge alcove, when something came up unexpectedly. Normally, with Jack, this kind of thing wouldn't arise. He turned to me – I was winding the wool for a mauve Guernsey, and Jack was picking his teeth with a library ticket – and he said, 'Chuckles', he said, 'what do you think to Women's Lib?' I was at a loss, which is very unusual for me. (When a burglar alarm went off in our crescent, and was mistaken for the four-minute warning, I was the only one who thought to cancel the milk.) Well, I've now ruminated on my position. I was unfortunately unable to get hold of a copy of *The Female Eunuch* by Germaine Greer, but I did read *Doctor in Clover* by Richard Gordon, which was the next book back on the left. So I'm not much further on in my research into Women's Lib, but I have found out what a sputum cup's for.

Girls – about this burning of bras we keep hearing about. *(Very loudly:)* A: *(To member of audience:)* No, not you, darling, you carry on. A: Some would say you don't get a decent jelly unless you put it in a mould. And B: There's nothing nastier than the smell of scorched elastic. What it boils down to is this – men and women were put on this earth for different purposes. A man is designed to walk three miles in the rain to phone for help when the car breaks down – and a woman is designed to say 'you took your time' when he comes back dripping wet.

No – that's just my lighthearted way of saying we girls are genetically programmed to rinse those dusters. Let's face it, if God had meant men to have children, he would have given them PVC aprons.

No time for more, unfortunately. Next week I shall be discussing politics, international terrorism, the unemployment figures, and how to make attractive earrings out of kidney stones. Till then, good evening.

Cosmetic Surgery

Little shop. A dim girl is behind the counter. Enter a female customer.

Girl   Can I help you?
Customer   I saw your advert.
Girl   Oh right. Well, the paraffin heater's nearly new.
Customer   No, the cosmetic surgery advert.
Girl   Oh, in the butcher's window? Sorry. Have a seat. Right.

Gets out bloodstained order book.

Don't worry, that's liver. Now, have you been to us before?
Customer   No.
Girl   Thought not, as you're not limping or visibly mutilated.
Customer   You mean things can go wrong?
Girl   Well, not every time. It's just that Mr Heathbury, the surgeon – do you know him? – he used to be Heathbury's Plumbing and Gasfitting, in the High St, he's got the drinker's disease, delirium, what is it, delirium …
Customer   Tremens?
Girl   Yeah, when you shake. But it's all right, we keep everything very blunt, to be on the safe side. And I'm for ever bringing him in a coffee.
Customer   Into the operating theatre? But doesn't everything have to be sterilised?
Girl   The milk's sterilised. I think that's why he does so many breast operations, you know, somewhere to put his doughnut. So, what was you after having? Only I must tell you Mr Heathbury doesn't do the below-the-waist, you know, the married organs. We don't do sex-changes.
Customer   Why not?
Girl   Well, we've had a lot of trouble with a Mr Brearley, who,

you know, wanted the full conversion job, pipes re-laid, all on-site rubbish removed. And he's been round here several times since, getting very unpleasant in a pinafore dress, complaining he still can't get the top C on 'Midnight in the Oasis'. So we just do the basics now, facial hair.

Customer Removal?

Girl No, we don't do removals.

Customer Do you remove facial hair?

Girl Not properly. We can tint it for you. We do breast augmentation, providing we've just done a breast reduction and that we have the right bits left over. We do apronectomy, you know, removing the stomach flesh of overweight people, that's very popular. In fact, we've had to hire a skip.

Customer Do you do nose jobs?

Girl Yes we do two. A big blobby one and a sort of little pointy one.

Customer Why?

Girl Those are the only ones he can do.

Customer I was wondering – I've lost a lot of weight, I could do with having all the loose skin removed, here.

Girl Yes, we've done that before. The lady came out with lovely upper arms, very tight skin. It was just if she went out in the sun, she had to prick them with a fork.

Customer I'll leave it for now.

Girl OK.

The girl stands up; she's got three legs.

Customer Good heavens!

Girl I know, isn't it awful – I can't resist, it's the staff discount.

The Reporter

A cheerful young girl reporter rings the front door bell: the door is answered by a weeping widow.

Reporter Widow Smith? I'm from the *Herald and Argus*. I believe your husband's just died and he was quite well known or something.
Widow Yes.
Reporter We thought we'd do a little piece on him, just a few inches.
Widow I'm not sure.
Reporter It's just there haven't been any jumble sales this week – we're a bit strapped.
Widow Come in then, I haven't done much tidying up, since …

They go in.

Reporter Good excuse, a death, isn't it, to bunk off the housework? If somebody dropped dead in our house, I'd be quite pleased.
Widow Would you like a drink?
Reporter Depends what he died of. If it's anything catching, I won't bother, ta.
Widow It was his heart. It was very sudden. Biscuit?
Reporter No, ta. Tried my bikini on last night, nearly had a heart attack.

She picks up a photo.

This him? He looks quite sick on this actually, doesn't he?

Tears from the widow.

	He looks a dead nice bloke, though. So – he did what exactly, drop dead?
Widow	He collapsed in front of the television.
Reporter	What channel?
Widow	ITV, I think. A 'Carry On' film.
Reporter	Oh, I love them. You didn't tape it, did you? Did he topple grotesquely out of the chair or anything?
Widow	Just slumped sideways. He spilt his coffee.
Reporter	It's left a nasty stain – I bet you could have killed him when you saw that. And he wrote, what, books, was it?
Widow	Thrillers. The 'Captain Black' stories.
Reporter	They're full of glamorous women, aren't they?
Widow	That's right.
Reporter	Who did he draw them from, then? Did he do a lot of sleeping around, because if he did it's no wonder he dropped dead, really.
Butch	*(off)* Hello?

Butch enters, a large insensitive man.

Reporter	In here, Butch! This is our photographer. This is the grieving widow, Butch. Husband popped off while watching a 'Carry On' film.
Butch	Great, love. Is he here? Can we prop him up somewhere, love?
Widow	No, he's …
Butch	Not to worry. Have you got a bikini, love? Thigh boots, hot pants?
Widow	No.
Butch	Does this wall come down?

Butch kicks it.

Reporter	He did spill his coffee in the throes of death, apparently.
Butch	Yeah, that might do. Hang on.

He chucks some tea on the rug.

That should show up better. Now, if you hold this up with one hand, love, and sort of point to the stain, do me a face love, a bit disgusted, a bit sort of rueful, like 'how the heck am I going to get this stain out', kind of thing. Can you just hop up on the telly for me?

She climbs up; he sweeps all of the ornaments off the top.

Just move these a sec – you'll have to crouch down a bit for me, just cup your chin, sort of 'me husband's popped his clogs but life goes on' kind of thing. Can you stop crying – I'm getting a bounce-off.

Reporter We could call it 'Carry On Crying', Butch.

Butch Great, fabulous. Thanks very much love, if you want any prints, just pop in to the office.

The reporter and Butch leave. The widow begins to take an overdose. The reporter comes back in.

Reporter Did I leave my ... stop, don't take any more. Butch! Quickly!

Butch comes back in.

Butch Oh that's smashing, love. Just turn the bottle round to me, love, then I can see the label, that's fabulous. Now hold me a pill up, and can you look sort of 'I'm topping myself but I can still have a laugh about it', kind of thing. Now take another and hitch your skirt up ...

Young Love: Two

Gail Carl?
Carl What?
Gail Do you know the facts of life?
Carl Some of them.
Gail Which ones do you know?
Carl Gravy. I know how that's made. I know where my mam's apron is.
Gail Do you know where babies come from?
Carl 'Course I do. They come from women.
Gail Yeah, but how come?
Carl Don't ask me. You want to send off for a pamphlet.
Gail What's that?
Carl They tell you what's what. We've got one at home about lagging.
Gail Well, can I not just read yours then, and not send off?
Carl No, you want a, er, wotsit pamphlet.
Gail What?
Carl You know – 'at it'. What is it you want to know anyway?
Gail Well it were something me mam said about my honeymoon.
Carl What?
Gail She said I've not to wear my pixie-hood in bed. She said men don't like it.
Carl Won't bother me.
Gail Will it not, Carl? And you know I always sleep in a pac-a-mac.
Carl So what?
Gail Do you really not mind, Carl?
Carl Why should I? I'm not going to be there, am I?
Gail In the honeymoon?
Carl Well, it's the money, in't it, Gail? We can't both go. You go this year, I'll go next.
Gail All right, Carl.

Pause.

Gail Carl?
Carl What?
Gail What's your favourite sandwich?
Carl Treacle.
Gail Just treacle?
Carl And bread.
Gail Mine's not.
Carl What?
Gail Treacle.

Pause.

Carl?
Carl What?
Gail Don't you want to know what my favourite sandwich is?
Carl Nope. That's your feminine mystiquery, that.
Gail What?
Carl Not knowing.
Gail What else do you not want to know?
Carl I don't want to know where to catch a bus for Haslingden.
Gail OK, Carl.

On Campus

Film. A modern university campus. Selina walks uncertainly round holding a piece of paper and a musical instrument in a case. She goes inside the Music Department.

Selina *(Voice Over)* I'm partly wanting to go to university for the education, and also for the social life. Just the words, 'on campus', they just have such an exciting sound.

TITLE 'ON CAMPUS'

Selina waits outside a door marked 'Music Auditions', the door opens, she grimaces at the camera and goes in. We hear the beginning of what is possibly a violin solo.

The audition room. Selina is playing for a panel of three elderly and middle-aged judges. She is playing 'Ebb Tide' on a Casio electronic miniature keyboard, very solemnly, with the sheet music on a music stand.

Selina comes out of the room, shaking.

Male Interviewer *(Voice Over)* How did you get on?
Selina It was very hard, much tougher than I imagined. Loads of questions about people I've never heard of. Johann Sebastian somebody … I just don't know … I think I played 'Ebb Tide' as well as I've ever played it. Fingers crossed.

The halls of residence. Cars pulling up. Parents and girl students carrying gear in. Camera follows Selina and her parents as they carry in a chest freezer.

Selina's room.

Selina	Just stick it down here for now, Daddy. I don't know where it should go till I get my Simon Rattle posters up.
Mummy	Lovely view of the tower, darling.
Selina	That's where everybody commits suicide apparently. It was in the prospectus. Look, I'll sort all this lot out, you go.
Mummy	All right, lambkin. Oh, Daddy's bought you a little present.
Daddy	It's just some marijuana, something to hand round. The girl in the shop seemed to think it was the right sort.
Selina	I don't know if people smoke it any more, Daddy, it's not like when you were at college.
Daddy	Well, I don't know, just chuck it in the bin if you don't want it. Have you got a bin?
Selina	Yes! Honestly, look, I'll be fine, do go, honestly.

Ad-lib farewells and kisses. Parents leave. Selina stands by the window, a tear in her eye.

Interviewer *(Voice Over)* Homesick?
Selina Well, it's all a bit strange, that's all. Room seems quite small now we've got the freezer in. I've never lived away from home before. Well, I've been grape-picking, but that was in our conservatory – didn't have to go abroad or anything ...

Noise of girls outside.

Suppose I'd better go and introduce myself, meet my mates. Sorry – can I just squeeze ...?

Hilary's room. Hilary and Selina sitting on the bed rather self-consciously, drinking coffee. Hilary has acne, wide thighs and speaks in funny voices.

Hilary I've brought my guitar, so any peculiar wailing noises you hear through the wall, it'll be me! Little me! Not so little, unfortunately.

Selina	I play 'Ebb Tide' actually, on an electronic keyboard. So if you fancy the odd duet …
Hilary	The odd duet! Very odd, if we're playing!
Selina	Wonder how much coffee we're going to drink before the end of term.
Hilary	Gallons. Gallons and galloons. In fact, I have to go to the loo, the lavatree. Excuse me a mo!
Selina	I think she and I will be pretty good mates. That's Hilary – she's doing religious studies and her second subject is netball, I think. She got here a day early so she's going to show me the spin drier and the milk machine.

Hilary comes back in.

Hilary	There's a place to dry tights across the way – if drying tights turns you on!
Selina	Er – your zip's undone.
Hilary	Whoops! That settles it. Back on the old diet. Can't have the boyfriend going off me.
Selina	What does he do?
Hilary	He's at school. Head boy, but we don't talk about that.
Selina	You're not really fat anyway.
Hilary	My hero!

Hilary's room.

Interviewer *(Voice Over)* So where are you off to tonight?

Selina	Well, tonight's the last night of Freshers' week, so everyone in Blakers, that's Blakethorpe Hall, we're all going to Peewee, that's Peabody Tower next door. And we're all having a sort of 'do' in the television room – so if anyone wants to watch television that's jolly hard cheese. And we all have to dress a little bit crazily – not difficult for me. So I've borrowed this rugby shirt from a rather nice mech. eng. student called Nick, and I'm wearing my school hat, just bash it up a bit – so I'll probably miss my first tutorial. I think this part of the film'd better be X certificate.

TV room seen through window. A few wimpish students with tinsel in their hair are doing folk dancing. Hilary is on one side having a miserable time.

The Music Department. Selina is walking along the corridor.

Selina   I think I thought everyone in the Music Department would be more stuffy – really sort of classically orientated. But everyone's really loony like me. We've got a wind ensemble, and there's a really crazy string quintet with would you believe, two cellos! And I've started a – well it's a pop group. We'll probably start doing gigs quite soon, I should think.

A practice room. Selina on the keyboard, girl on the recorder, and two weedy boys on the oboe and the viola, are nearing the end of 'Copacabana', which they are playing very slowly and rigidly.

Selina   I think we really got somewhere with it that time. I liked the little *legato* bit you did before the double *forte*, Robin – very effective, wasn't it, Tanya? Phew, I'm whacked. Where's the Party Four?

Music. Tracking shot past all the lit-up windows of the hall of residence. There is a girl at each window studying by the light of an Anglepoise. At Hilary's window we see her squeezing her spots and eating the last but one of a box of Mr Kipling's Bakewell Fingers.

Hall of Residence. Corridor. Selina and other girls are giggling and closing the lift doors.

Selina   We've just put all Hilary's furniture into the lift; and then we're going to jam the doors. Get lost, she's coming.

They scatter as Hilary approaches, in netball skirt and hockey boots.

Communal kitchen. Food lockers and Baby Bellings. Selina and friend Maggie are heating tomato soup. Maggie unwraps crumby packet of Anchor.

Maggie   Some twerp's been at my butter. Bet it was Hilary.
Selina   Maggie!
Maggie   Well, I bet it would have been if she hadn't … God knows how they ever got her on the stretcher, legs that size.
Selina   Shut up, Maggie.
Interviewer   *(Voice Over)* Do you think you had anything to do with Hilary's suicide attempt?
Both   No, not really, did we?
Selina   I think going away to university for the first time, it's a strain on anybody, the lectures, making your own coffee, buying soap-powder, there's a lot of pressure. And if you're fat and ugly with a hopeless personality, you're probably better off taking an overdose or something.
Interviewer   So you're not badly affected by this business with Hilary?
Selina   I might have been when I first came, but not now. I've been here ten days and I can cope. Actually, it's great that her room's empty, because I've got somewhere to put my freezer.

Shoe Shop

The assistant is a smiling, mad, middle-aged woman.
A customer enters.

Customer Hello, there's a pair of shoes in the window.
Assistant That's right. We do that because it's a shoe shop.
Customer They're black lace-ups, fifteen ninety-nine.
Assistant Are they?
Customer Yeah, can I try them on?
Assistant On your feet?
Customer Yes.
Assistant All right, why not?

She blunders into the window and comes back with any old pair.

Customer No, sorry, the black ones, they're a flat lace-up.
Assistant Beg pardon?
Customer Those aren't flat.

She breaks the heels off.

Assistant Flatter now.
Customer But they're red.
Assistant They are quite red, aren't they?
Customer I want a black pair.
Assistant I know. I can never get what I want when I go shopping.
Customer They're in the window.
Assistant Are they?

She runs into the window.

Get out! Get out! We think we've got hens in the
skirting-board. We found droppings by the pop-sox. I

think they're droppings. Mrs Brinsley says they're Janine's liquorice allsorts – she won't eat the black ones. Now what was it you wanted?

Customer   Not these, I want the black ones.

Assistant   They've been swept up. You don't think someone might come in asking for hen-droppings in a shoe-shop.

Customer   Hen droppings are white – sheep droppings are black.

Assistant   I don't think we've got sheep in the skirting-board, unless they're breeding them very small. They may be, with Lady Helen Windsor setting a trend for fingerless gloves.

Customer   Can I try on the black lace-ups in the window?

Assistant   Well you can, but everyone in the street will be able to see you.

Customer   Can you get them in my size and I'll try them on here?

Assistant   All right, we're not busy.

Customer   I'm five and a half.

Assistant   You're very tall, do you take vitamins?

Customer   My shoe size is five and a half. Do you have the black lace-ups in that size?

Assistant   We might have.

Customer   Can you go in the stockroom?

Assistant   Yeah, I can go anywhere here, toilets, backyard, they're very free and easy ...

She goes off, singing 'Look at me, I'm as helpless as a kitten up a tree'. Comes back with the shoes.

Are these the ones?

Customer   Yes.

Assistant   I don't like them.

Customer   What?

Assistant   Because I know this woman, and she has a pair and she got knocked down by an industrial tribunal, and the doctor says she's to wear ponchos.

Customer   I haven't got a poncho.

Assistant   Neither had she. We did a sponsored crochet but she moved to Norwich.

Customer   They're a bit tight.

Assistant   Janine? Can I have your shoe horn please?

Janine chucks it over. The assistant scratches her back with it and chucks it back.

	Ta. What were you saying?
Customer	No, they're too small.
Assistant	You're like me, broadfooted – and are you a Taurus and can't stick cabbage?
Customer	No.
Assistant	You're not like me, then. Look, you better go. They don't like me sitting down and talking in shop hours.
Customer	Couldn't I try a bigger size?
Assistant	No, I'm in enough trouble as it is. You come in here asking for hen droppings, you want to get changed in the window – this is a shoe shop not a soft porn video merchant's, and I should know because my husband runs one. Well, he's not my husband, but he rubbed up against me in a sports jacket so he's as good as. And it's no good offering me used notes and trips to Bermuda because I've got a rare skin disease and can't go in the sun without a *Woman's Realm* on my head. So you can stuff it because I know my rights; I voted Conservative but the chappy didn't get in because lots of people round here had to stay in and watch television that night, and I never wanted free milk anyway, I'm allergic – sores run in our family.

Girl goes. Janine wanders over.

Janine	Wrong size?
Assistant	Yes, she was like me, broadfooted.

Dandruff Commercial

Actress All through the winter, right, I didn't seem to have dandruff at all, then I went on holiday, because I know this married man, and his wife thought he was away working, blah, blah ... usual thing.

So there we were, lots of sex and everything, sun – and I got really brown, and we're lying on the beach one day, and John said, that's not his real name, because he's quite well known ... and John said, 'Hey, what are those white specks on your leg?', and I look down, and I had all this terrible dandruff, all round the tops of my legs. Like really obvious with my tan – and it was like, you know, bikini dandruff. Like really a turn-off for him, and it was a problem for me, because if I don't sleep with him I don't get my rent paid, anyway, so then a friend said, why not paint your legs white ... and I said like, why don't you mind your own business, 'cos I was, you know, fairly narked by this time.

Anyway – then another friend said why not try – dadah! – the new shampoo, your shampoo, and it was great, really fabulous – dandruff went by about third day, it left a few scars and it rotted my pants but on the whole, I'm really pleased, yes ...

Toddlers

Victoria and Julie dressed as toddlers – woolly hats, etc – in two swings. The kind with bars at the front. Front blank, they swing gently for some time.

Julie   Thought of any jokes for this sketch yet?
Victoria Nope.

They carry on swinging.

The Practice Room

A stuffy music student is practising something fiddly and classical on the piano. Enter a beaming chain-smoking cleaner; she stands listening to the pianist making mistakes.

Cleaner Having trouble, are you?

Pianist Yes, a little.

Cleaner Music like that – it's all the same whether you play it wrong or not, isn't it? Do you not know any proper tunes?

Pianist I'm sorry?

Cleaner Do you know 'Dream of Olwen'? Lovely that. That were on in Women's Surgical the night I had my cervix cauterised. Tell you what – do us the 'Harry Lime Theme' *(hums a bit).* Great that. Now, that's dead easy – my Uncle Albert could play it and he had a metal plate in his head.

Pianist I'm sorry.

Cleaner No, you're all right. Quite a blessing, really. If he sat with his back to the aerial we could get Welsh television. Back inside now, poor old thing. Shoplifting. Caught outside Tesco's with half a pound of skinless links stuffed down his trousers. That caused a certain amount of confusion as well – he was nearly had up on two charges. *(Picking up concert programme off the piano:)* Go to concerts a lot, do you?

Pianist When I can, yes.

Cleaner Yeah, smashing. Ever see Renato do 'Moonlight Sonata'?

Pianist No, I don't think …

Cleaner On roller skates with the xylophone strapped round his neck. Finished up in a wicker basket whistling 'Colonel Bogey' while a woman in a sequined bra thrust spears through all parts of his body.

Pianist Gosh. I suppose he escaped unscathed?

Cleaner No, he bled to death, actually. There was some kind of a mix-up over who was working the trap-door. *(Drops ash inside piano.)*

Pianist	Er, I don't think the principal would think that was terribly good for the Steinway.
Cleaner	Tough titty. He's lucky Mrs Harris is off sick. She always says what's the point dragging round to the toilet when there's timps handy. No, I'm only kidding. It were only an old French horn.
Pianist	I must get on, actually.
Cleaner	I see that Janet Baker were here last week.
Pianist	Yes, it was marvellous. We could hear her practising in number seven.
Cleaner	Ooh, so could we. There's me trying to listen to 'Mystery Voice' on the wireless. In the end I knocked on the door, I said for God's sake put a sock in it or give us something a bit more cheerful. I told her, I said you'd get booed off down the British Legion, you would. I said call yourself a music lover? She didn't know nothing – 'Tie a Yellow Ribbon', 'Bright Eyes' …
Pianist	Well, I must persevere …
Cleaner	Don't mind me, you carry on. Having lessons, are you?
Pianist	Yes. Professor Hartley. *(Bum note.)*
Cleaner	Ask him for a refund. *(Laughs.)* No, I'm only kidding. I tell you a lovely pianist could learn you a few things – Bobby Crush. He can cross his hands over and everything. Lovely smile. Going to turn pro?
Pianist	I like to think so, one day.
Cleaner	Hey – I know. They're looking for someone down the snug at the Winston. Good job – £5 a night and any ploughman's they've left over from dinnertime. It wouldn't have fell vacant, but some of the lads got a bit tanked up and tried to jam pianist's head in the lid. It were a scream. Anyway shall I put a word in for you?
Pianist	Quite honestly, I do aspire a little higher than the snug.
Cleaner	What, the lounge? *(Doubtful.)* Well, maybe. They do more your classical stuff – 'Lara's Theme', 'Edelweiss' …
Pianist	I won't be able to get a job anywhere if I don't get this right.
Cleaner	You know what you're doing wrong?
Pianist	What?
Cleaner	Well, that dotted semi-quaver is tied over the bar, and the middle note of the triplet isn't accidental. *(Leaving.)* And another thing – your nails need cutting.

Supermarket Checkout

An impatient woman customer is having her groceries checked out by a slow girl on the till. She looks at a packet of bacon.

Till girl   It's got no price on. Did you notice how much they were?
Customer No, I didn't.

She looks round and holds up the bacon.

Till girl   Won't be long.
Customer Good.

Long pause.

Till girl   We're a bit short-handed today. Us that works here gets the old food cheap, and if it's something like a pork pie, you can actually die, apparently. So the girl that checks the prices, she's probably, you know, passed on.
Customer Honestly, I thought you girls on the tills knew all the prices.
Till girl   I've only come on the till today. I was in meat packing before, then an overall came free so I come here.
Customer But surely you wear an overall when you're packing meat?
Till girl   No, you must bring something from home. I had our dog's blanket.
Customer You can't have dogs in a place where food is prepared.
Till girl   I didn't. It's dead. It were called Whiskey. It ate one of the pork pies from here.
Customer But you do wear gloves, don't you, when you're wrapping meat?
Till girl   I did, woolly ones. I get a lot of colds, I like to have something to wipe my nose on. I liked it in the meat-packing department, it were dead near the toilet.

Customer	Well it sounds disgusting. Who's in charge of that department?
Till girl	Mr Waterhouse. He's not here. He goes to some sort of a special clinic on Thursdays. I'll do your veg, anyway.

She coughs and splutters all over it.

Sorry. I've caught this cold off Susan on smoked meats. They're not smoked when they come, but she's on sixty a day.

Customer	It's all over the cauliflower.
Till girl	Sorry.

She wipes it on her overall.

Corned beef, ninety-eight. It's funny how much tins can actually blow out without bursting, isn't it?

Customer	You can't sell a blown tin.
Till girl	We can, they're dead popular.
Customer	Oh look, how much longer is this going to take?
Till girl	Do you want me to ask the supervisor?
Customer	Yes, thank you.

The till girl speaks into intercom.

Till girl	Hello?
Intercom	Hello?
Till girl	Hello, Mrs Brinsley, it's Gemma here.
Intercom	Hello Gemma, nice to talk to you.
Till girl	Nice to talk to you, Mrs Brinsley. How's your boils?
Intercom	Worse.
Till girl	So putting you on the cheese counter hasn't helped? Well, what I'm calling about, I've a lady here, and she's brought me a packet of bacon with no price.
Intercom	Is it streaky?
Till girl	Well, it is a bit but it'll probably wash off.

She wipes it with filthy dishcloth.

The sell-by-date is 5 August 1984. No, hang on.

She scrapes something off.

1964.

Intercom	Three and nine.
Till girl	Three and nine, thank you.
Customer	You mean that bacon's twenty years old?
Till girl	I don't know. I was away when we did addings. *(She finishes checking out the rest of the stuff.)*
Customer	This place is a disgrace – filthy, unhygienic, the food's not safe to eat, the staff are all positively diseased.
Till girl	That's two pounds seventy-one pence, please.
Customer	On the other hand, it's very cheap and easy to park. Bye.

Kitty: One

Kitty is about fifty-three, from Manchester and proud of it. She speaks as she finds and knows what's what. She is sitting in a small bare studio, on a hard chair. She isn't nervous.

Kitty   Good evening. My name's Kitty. I've had a boob off and I can't stomach whelks so that's me for you. I don't know why I've been asked to interrupt your viewing like this, but I'm apparently something of a celebrity since I walked the Pennine Way in slingbacks in an attempt to publicise Mental Health. They've asked me to talk about aspects of life in general, nuclear war, peg-bags …

I wasn't going to come today, actually. I'm not a fan of the modern railway system. I strongly object to paying twenty-seven pounds fifty to walk the length and breadth of the train with a sausage in a plastic box. But they offered me a chopper from Cheadle so here I am.

I'm going to start with the body – you see I don't mince words. Time and again I'm poked in the street by complete acquaintances – Kitty, they say to me, how do you keep so young, do you perhaps inject yourself with a solution deriving from the placenta of female gibbons? Well, no, I say, I don't, as it happens. I'm blessed with a robust constitution, my father's mother ran her own abbatoir, and I've only had the need of hospitalisation once – that's when I was concussed by an electric potato peeler at the Ideal Home Exhibition.

No, the secret of my youthful appearance is simply – mashed swede. As a face-mask, as a night cap, and in an emergency, as a draught-excluder. I do have to be careful about my health, because I have a grumbling ovary which once flared up in the middle of *The Gondoliers*. My three rules for a long life are regular exercise, hobbies and complete avoidance of midget gems.

I'm not one for dance classes, feeling if God had wanted us to wear leotards he would have painted us purple. I have a system of elastic loops dangling from the knob of my cistern cupboard. It's just a little thing I knocked up from some old knicker waistbands. I string up before breakfast and I can exert myself to Victor Sylvester till the cows come home.

There's also a rumour going round our block that I play golf. Let me scotch it. I do have what seems to be a golf-bag on my telephone table but it's actually a pyjama-case made by a friend who has trouble with her nerves in Buckinghamshire.

Well, I can't stop chatting, much as I'd like to – my maisonette backs onto a cake factory, so I'm dusting my knick-knacks all the day long.

And I shall wait to see myself before I do any more. Fortunately, I've just had my TV mended. I say mended – a shifty young man in plimsolls waggled my aerial and wolfed my Gipsy Creams, but that's the comprehensive system for you.

I must go, I'm having tea with the boys in flat five. They're a lovely couple of young men, and what they don't know about Mikhail Barishnikov is nobody's business. So I'd better wrap up this little gift I've got them. It's a gravy boat in the shape of Tony Hancock – they'll be thrilled.

She peers round the studio.

Now, who had hold of my showerproof? It's irreplaceable, you know, being in tangerine poplin, which apparently there's no call for ...

She gets up and walks past the camera.

There's a mauve pedestal mat of mine, too.

Young Love: Three

Gail Carl?

Carl What?

Gail Would you rather have a red washing-up bowl and a red washing-up bowl, brush I mean, or a brown washing-up brush, I mean bowl, and a brown washing-up brush, or a yellow washing-up bowl and a brown washing-up brush?

Carl Why?

Gail Just wondered.

Carl We want to be investing in paintings, us.

Gail Picture paintings?

Carl Yeah. Something with elephants.

Gail I don't really like elephants, Carl.

Carl Well, you say what's to be on t'painting, then.

Gail I know, let's have a painting of digestive biscuits, 'cos we both like them don't we, Carl?

Carl No, it's got to be something like some scenery.

Gail All right, then, some digestive biscuits and a Alp.

Carl All right, but they better be chocolate.

Gail Why are they called Alps, Carl?

Carl Well, people go ski-ing on them, and fall off, don't they? And they go 'Help Help' but it sounds like 'Alp' 'cos they all have ear-muffs on.

Gail You're dead clever, you. You should have gone to – where is it, they have scarves?

Carl Oxford and Cambridge.

Gail Yeah, you should have gone there.

Carl For three years?

Gail Yeah.

Carl And lose all t'good-will on the window-cleaning?

Gail Never thought of that, Carl.

This House Believes

Schoolgirl Mr Chairman, Lords, Ladies and Gentlemen, I am speaking to oppose the motion 'This house believes that school uniform should be abolished'. Oh, so this house believes that school uniform should be abolished, does it? Does it really think it's a good idea for everybody to come to school wearing exactly what they please? I think we should see some pretty funny sights, don't you?

But to be serious for a moment or two, let us first examine the history of school uniform in some detail. If you care to look at the Bayeux tapestry, which I think everyone would agree is pretty old, you will see that nearly everyone on that tapestry is wearing uniform – and of course there are many other examples of this.

But to bring us right up to date, I think we can do no better than look at the finest schools in our country today, – Eton, Winchester, Harrow, St John's School Leatherhead, where my brother goes – and see whether they wear uniform or not. They do. Lots of it. And I do not pick those schools out for snob reasons: plenty of ordinary people go to them, such as architects' children, and many leave and go into the music business, so you cannot say uniform has made them fuddy-duddy, as Derek Bainbridge would have had you believe previously.

All right then, let us picture a typical school day without uniform. Just suppose one catches two fourth years hanging round the Lower Corridor pegs at five to nine and one requests them to sign the Punishment Book. How are they to know I am a Punishment Monitor if I am not wearing my red Punishment Tie? In fact how can they tell I am a monitor at all if they can't see my monitor's cardigan as opposed to everyone else's pullover who's not a monitor? If this kind of thing were repeated all over the school I don't think we'd get much work done, do you?

But there is yet another side to this vexed question. Were we not to wear uniform, do you really want to have to get up earlier in order to choose what to wear? I, for one, don't want to stand dithering in front of eleven pairs of trousers keeping my mother waiting in the Range Rover, do you? But to take my analogy a stage further, Derek Bainbridge claims that the official uniform is expensive and a great strain on the parents of the poorer children. Well it seems to me if people's fathers took the trouble to pass exams in accountancy and business management like some people's fathers, they would have plenty of money for new blazers and other things such as holiday flatlets in Fuengirola. But I digress. And furthermore – if some people cannot be trusted to sign the Punishment Book without drawing private parts on it, I don't really think they can be trusted to dress suitably for school *do you*? I think we can all imagine what would happen if certain people arrived in backless sweaters only to find the heating was off due to education cuts. I think certain people would find they were crawling to other certain people to borrow their monitor's cardigans, don't you? A hypothesis which, as Hamlet said, is devoutly not to be wished.

Finally, to sum up, let me just give you three reasons why I think you should vote for me, against the motion.

One: I think school uniform promotes a sense of identity and team spirit.

Two: it prevents discrimination on the grounds of class and economic differences.

Three: my father is now the sole supplier of uniform to this school, and anyone who votes for me will get a discount.

Thank you.

Groupies

The dressing-room. Bella and Enid, two dim but beaming typists, with woolly hats, speech impediments and thick glasses, approach. The star, a thirty-nine-ish male singer, is relaxed but sweaty after the show.

Knock on door.

Star Come in. *(The girls stick their heads round the door.)*

Bella We just come round to say it were a really great show tonight. Really smashing, wasn't it?

Enid Yeah.

Bella Yeah. *(They beam at him.)*

Star Come in, girls.

Bella Are you not busy?

Star Never too busy to see the fans who've put me where I am today. *(They come in.)* So – you enjoyed the show? That's good.

Bella Oh it were great, wasn't it?

Enid Yeah.

Bella Yeah. Mind you, we're right easily pleased.

Star Would you like a signed photo *(indicating a pile on dressing-table)* ?

Bella Do we?

Enid No.

Bella No. We don't, thanks.

Star Oh – OK. Well, look girls …

Bella And I can't think of anybody else that would want one, can you?

Enid No.

Bella No, I can't. Everyone at the office thinks you're really dated.

Enid 'As-been. *(Laughs inanely.)*

Bella Except Mrs Singh.

Enid She's Indian.

Bella She'd never heard of you. Who is it she likes?

Enid	Max Jaffa.
Bella	That's right. *(They beam.)*
Star	Well look girls – I must be fair – I like to spend an equal amount of time with all my fans – I'm sure there must be quite a few waiting outside.
Bella	No there aren't, are there?
Enid	No.
Bella	No. In fact some people didn't even stop till the end. *(They laugh.)*
Star	There's nobody waiting?
Bella	No. Is there not?
Enid	No.
Bella	No.
Star	Most towns I play, to be frank – they're bursting the door down to get at me. Not just ordinary fans – you know, er, groupies.
Bella	That's us.
Star	Sorry?
Bella	We're the groupies. Aren't we?
Enid	Yeah.
Bella	Yeah, we are.
Star	I'm sorry, I'm not –
Bella	We do everyone that comes here. It's like our 'obby, isn't it?
Enid	Like rugs. Making rugs. 'Obby.
Star	And you're sure there's nobody else here?
Bella	No. Just us. What do you want doing?
Star	What kind of things do you normally do?
Bella	Whatever they ask for. Versatile, aren't we?
Enid	Whatever is asked for we will do.
Bella	They all have different things they want doing, don't they?
Enid	John Hanson.
Star	What did he want?
Bella	What were it?
Enid	Haddock.
Bella	And scallops.
Enid	On a tray. And a can of Vimto.
Bella	We've posted letters for Ivor Emmanuel.
Enid	Played Monopoly with Larry Grayson.
Star	But, girls – most groupies … I don't know how to put this.

Bella What?

Enid What?

Star Most groupies just want to sleep with – whoever it is.

Bella Do they? Larry Grayson never said nothing about that …

Enid What? Sex?

Star Well, yes …

Bella and **Enid** Oh …

Bella *(as they tear off their hats and coats)* Ooh I like the sound of that much better, don't you?

Enid Yeah.

Bella Yeah. I were bored stiff with Monopoly, weren't you?

Enid Yeah.

Bella Yeah. *(They have both stripped down to their liberty bodices, heavy duty bras etc.)* Right – which of us you want first?

The star resignedly begins to unbutton his shirt.

Margery and Joan: One

Margery is cooking. Joan is standing too close, watching.

Joan And that's just ordinary clear honey is it, Margery?

Margery Just ordinary clear honey, Joan – whoops, it does tend to go everywhere if you're not too careful.

Joan So the best thing is to *be* careful, Margery, or it will get everywhere – would that be right?

Margery Absolutely. Now, I'm taking my four ounces of flaked almonds from my nice little pottery bowl I bought in Malaga.

Joan What we'd call a Spanish bowl, then Margery?

Margery That's right, Joan, but of course if the viewers have never been to Spain – some of them are perhaps disabled or agoraphobic – an ordinary vinyl or plastic bowl will do just as well. Just scrape up those last few crumbs …

The bowl smashes on floor.

Joan My goodness, quite a noisy little bowl, Margery. Looks like you'll have to be flying back to Spain, Margery, to get another one, perhaps?

Margery Well, I'm unfortunately not able to fly, Joan, since the plane crash that killed my whole family, and in which I injured my pelvis.

Joan I'm glad you brought that up, Margery, because we'll be talking about fatal plane crashes and whether it's worth taking sandwiches next week. So see you then.

Fade in music, fade out dialogue.

And this is just plain evaporated milk, is it Margery?

Margery No, it's condensed.

Joan Condensed, I beg your pardon. Easy to muddle up, I

should think, especially if you have tunnel vision or are thinking of getting it ...

Film Classic

*Black-and-white film. Freda and Barry in belted raincoats are
under a viaduct in the rain. They are snogging. She breaks away.*

Freda Barry, no!
Barry By 'eck, I've never thought of myself as romantic, Freda, but
you've got a cracking bust.
Freda I've got to go, Barry, I'm on first shift down pit.
Barry Snog a bit longer and then catch last bus.
Freda I can't.
Barry I'll give you t'threepence.
Freda It's not the money. My mam's being buried tomorrow, and
I've got to mek t'sandwiches.
Barry Just a bit longer – I haven't finished unbuttoning your
cardigan yet.
Freda I'm not in the mood.
Barry What's up, love?

Pause.

Freda What do you think?

Pause.

Barry Oh no. How did it happen?
Freda You know flicking well how it happened.
Barry But we were dead careful.
Freda Not careful enough, Barry.
Barry Did you try gin?
Freda Yes.
Barry And hot baths?
Freda Yes! Shut up – it's no good.
Barry What am I going to tell me mam?
Freda You'll just have to tell her t'truth. The whippet got wet, caught
cold and died.

Service Wash

An old bag is folding clothes.

Old Bag I can remember when pants were pants. You wore them for twenty years, then you cut them down for pan scrubs. Or quilts. We used to make lovely quilts out of Celanese bloomers. Every gusset a memory. Not bras. They won't lie flat. We didn't wear bras till after the war, round here. We stayed in and polished the lino.

I didn't see an Oxo cube till I was twenty-five. That's when I got my glasses. And we weren't having hysterectomies every two minutes either, like the girls these days. If something went wrong down below, you kept your gob shut and turned up the wireless.

We never got woken with a teasmade. We were knocked up every morning by a man with a six-foot pole. It wasn't all fun. We'd no showers. We used to club together and send the dirtiest one to the Slipper Baths. We might have been mucky but we had clean slippers.

And it was all clogs. Clogs on cobbles – you could hardly hear yourself coughing up blood. Clogs – when times were hard we had them for every meal, with condensed milk, if we were lucky.

And no one had cars. If you wanted to get run over, you'd to catch a bus to the main road. And of course, corner shop was the only one with gas, so you'd to go cap in hand if you wanted to gas yourself.

For years we had to make our own rugs. We used to stitch mice on to pieces of sacking. We weren't always making

jokes either. I once passed a remark about parsnips and
couldn't sit down for a week.

Oh, but I shall never forget the Coronation. 1953. We all
crammed into the one front room and stared at this tiny
grey picture. Somebody had cut it out of the paper –
nobody got television till the year after.

I think we were more neighbourly. If anyone was ill in bed,
the whole street would let themselves in and ransack the
parlour.

And we didn't do all this keep-fit. We got our exercise
lowering coffins out of upstairs windows. In fact, if people
were very heavy we used to ask them to die downstairs.

It wasn't all gloom. My brother went to Spain, which was
very unusual in those days. Mind you, that was the Civil
War, and he got shot for trying to paddle.

We couldn't afford holidays. Sometimes us kids would take
some dry bread and a bottle of water and sit in the TB
clinic, but that was about it.

We had community spirit round here, right to the end. The
day they demolished our street it was like the war all over
again – dead bodies, hands sticking out of the rubble. The
council should have let us know.

That's me done, best be off. Got a bit of cellular blanket
for my supper, don't want it to spoil. Ta-ra …

The Boutique

A tiny dark boutique. A customer is by a rail of jeans. The assistant is up a ladder with a machine-gun and a walkie-talkie.

Customer   Excuse me, are you serving?

Assistant   I don't think we're actually supposed to serve people – just shoot them if they do something suspicious.

Customer   I just wondered if you had these in a different size?

Assistant   Hang on. *(Into her walkie-talkie:)* I'm going out on the floor, Eileen. There's no landmines in separates, are there? OK. If you have any trouble with people wanting to buy things, let the dogs out. *(Climbing down.)* Can I help you?

Customer   I wondered if you have these in a fourteen?

Assistant   You what? This is a boutique, not the Elephant House. *(Laughing up to a two-way mirror:)* Hey, Eileen, got another Fatso in – they never learn, do they? We don't do much above a size eight – I mean, it's so depressing for us, dealing with great wobbling lumps of flesh all day long.

Customer   So you haven't got anything in a size fourteen?

Assistant   They might have sent something by mistake. *(Riffles along rail.)* There's these.

Customer   I don't really suit green.

Assistant   I shouldn't think you suit much do you, body like that. I say 'body' … The day I go over six and a half stone, it's razor blades in the bath, d'you know what I mean? Do you want them, or not?

Customer   Could I try them on?

Assistant   Yeah, well don't break anything. We don't usually let obese people in the cubicles, in case they sweat on the wallpaper.

Customer   They look a bit small to me.

Assistant   It's up to you, Porky. *(Customer goes into cubicle.)* If they don't fit you, the only other thing in this shop that will is the cubicle curtains. They're supposed to be tight-fitting these days, you know. I don't suppose you go out much, do you, being so ugly? I have them that tight, I need surgery to get things out of my pockets. (*She whips back the curtain as the customer has them at the half-way-up stage.*) Hey, Eileen, get the Polaroid. Another one for the toilet wall. (*Customer closes curtain.*) Hey Eileen, Martin went out with someone fat once – eight stone or something she was – he said she was like a waterbed with legs.

The customer comes out in own clothes, puts the jeans in the assistant's hands and leaves.

I don't know why we bother being so pleasant.

Margery and Joan: Two

Joan	And, leaving Mr Dixon to get on with his model of Sheena Easton in dog food, we'll stroll over to Consumer Corner, to see what Margery's been buying today. Hello, Margery, you've been looking at what, this week, Margery?

Margery is at a table covered in sex aids, sprays, rubber balaclavas, etc.

Margery	Hello Joan. Many people these days are finding their private lives have gone a little bit flat, little bit uninteresting, so I've been looking at devices, attachments, in fact private sex gadgets in general.
Joan	Lovely. This looks rather nice, Margery – what's this for?
Margery	Yes it is rather nice, isn't it? It's just come on the market, Joan – it's an updating of the old hand-held partner stimulator. It's electronic, and the two vibrating pads here are covered in wipeable Dralon-effect, and what I like very much is the extra socket on the side if there should happen to be a group of you, and you need just that little bit more power.
Joan	So it's practical as well as being a nice thing to have around the house?
Margery	Absolutely. Now, I was very interested in this –
Joan	That looks like an ordinary personal massager, Margery, what's so special about it?
Margery	What's special about it, Joan, is that not only is it half the price of a conventional rubbing unit, it folds up, and can be slipped into a spectacle case or luncheon-voucher holder.
Joan	So it can go virtually anywhere, Margery?
Margery	Virtually anywhere, Joan.
Joan	So if it's high summer, I'm crossing the River Avon by ferry, I'm in a sleeveless dress, I haven't a shopping bag with me ...?

Margery   You can slip it into the pocket of your cardi, or even into the top of your sock.

Joan   Well I don't wear socks myself, but from our large postbag, I know lots of our viewers do, and next week we'll be delving into that all-important question, What do we do with socks that have got dirty? Bye.

Margery begins to demonstrate a drop-down rubber bra that lights up ...

Giving Notes

Alma, a middle-aged sprightly woman, addresses her amateur company after a rehearsal of Hamlet. *She claps her hands.*

Alma   Right. Bit of hush please. Connie! Thank you. Now that was quite a good rehearsal; I was quite pleased. There were a few raised eyebrows when we let it slip the Piecrust Players were having a bash at Shakespeare but I think we're getting there. But I can't say this too often: it may be *Hamlet* but it's got to be Fun Fun Fun!

She consults her notes.

Now we're still very loose on lines. Where's Gertrude? I'm not so worried about you – if you 'dry' just give us a bit of business with the shower cap. But Barbara – you will have to buckle down. I mean, Ophelia's mad scene, 'There's rosemary, that's for remembrance' – it's no good just bunging a few herbs about and saying, 'Don't mind me, I'm a loony'. Yes? You see, this is our marvellous bard, Barbara, you cannot paraphrase. It's not like Pinter where you can more or less say what you like as long as you leave enough gaps.

Right, Act One, Scene One, on the ramparts. Now I know the whist table is a bit wobbly, but until Stan works out how to adapt the Beanstalk it'll have to do. What's this? Atmosphere? Yes – now what did we work on, Philip? Yes, it's midnight, it's jolly cold. What do we do when it's cold? We go 'Brrr', and we do this (*slaps hands on arms*). Right, well don't forget again, please. And cut the hot-water bottle, it's not working.

Where's my ghost of Hamlet's father? Oh yes, what went wrong tonight, Betty? He's on nights still, is he? OK. Well, it's not really on for you to play that particular part, Betty – you're already doing the Player Queen and the back legs of Hamlet's donkey. Well, we don't know he didn't have one, do we? Why waste a good cossy?

Hamlet – drop the Geordie, David, it's not coming over. Your characterisation's reasonably good, David, but it's just far too gloomy. Fair enough, make him a little bit depressed at the beginning, but start lightening it from Scene Two, from the hokey-cokey onwards, I'd say. And perhaps the, er, 'Get thee to a nunnery' with Ophelia – perhaps give a little wink to the audience, or something, because he's really just having her on, isn't he, we decided …

Polonius, try and show the age of the man in your voice and in your bearing, rather than waving the bus-pass. I think you'll find it easier when we get the walking frame. Is that coming, Connie? OK.

The Players' scene: did any of you feel it had stretched a bit too … ? Yes. I think we'll go back to the tumbling on the entrance, rather than the extract from *Barnum*. You see, we're running at six hours twenty now, and if we're going to put those soliloquies back in …

Gravediggers? Oh yes, gravediggers. The problem here is that Shakespeare hasn't given us a lot to play with – I feel we're a little short on laughs, so Harold, you do your dribbling, and Arthur, just put in anything you can remember from the Ayckbourn, yes?

The mad scene: apart from lines, much better, Barbara – I can tell you're getting more used to the straitjacket. Oh – any news on the skull, Connie? I'm just thinking, if your little dog pulls through, we'll have to fall back on papier mâché. All right, Connie, as long as it's dead by the dress …

Oh yes, Hamlet, Act Three, Scene One, I think that cut works very well, 'To be or not to be', then Ophelia comes straight in, it moves it on, it's more pacey …

Act Five, Gertrude, late again. What? Well, is there no service wash? I'm sure Dame Edith wasn't forever nipping out to feed the dryer.

That's about it – oh yes, Rosencrantz and Guildenstern, you're not on long, make your mark. I don't think it's too gimmicky, the tandem. And a most important general note – make up! Half of you looked as if you hadn't got any on! And Claudius – no moles again? (*Sighs*.) I bet Margaret Lockwood never left hers in the glove compartment.

That's it for tonight then; thank you. I shall expect you to be word-perfect by the next rehearsal. Have any of you realised what date we're up to? Yes, April the twenty-seventh! And when do we open? August! It's not long!

Cleaning

A large, messy, stripped-pine kitchen. Ursula, a large messy lady novelist in a smock sits drinking tea with Kent, a disdainful Northern man.

Ursula   You know, it's amazing: you're the only person who's answered the advert. I just cannot get a cleaner. I'm afraid it's all rather neglected in here.

Kent   Well, yes, I was just admiring that blue mink hat, but I see now it's a mouldy pizza.

Ursula   I'm a novelist, and it's so hard to do everything. Is the tea all right?

Kent   Not really.

Ursula   Oh sorry, is it too strong?

Kent   I'm just a bit perturbed by the way it's taken the tarnish off this teaspoon.

Ursula   Biscuit?

Kent   Have they got chemicals in?

Ursula   Preservatives?

Kent   I was hoping for disinfectant.

Ursula   No, I baked them myself.

Kent   I bet Mr Kipling's worried.

Ursula   Aren't you going to finish it?

Kent   I'll keep it by me – you never know, I may need to force a lock.

Pause.

Anyone ever told you you've got a look of Molly Weir?

Ursula   No.

Kent   I'm not surprised.

Ursula   Have you been a cleaner for long?

Kent   Well, I was abroad for some years.

Ursula   Really?

Kent	Lived with Picasso, actually.
Ursula	The painter?
Kent	Yes. I had a put-u-up in the back bedroom. I had to come away. It was nice, but, you know, everything tasted of turps. Henry Moore was the same – a stranger to Harpic.
Ursula	You obviously know a lot about cleaning.
Kent	I was approached by 'Mastermind' to set the questions for the specialised subject 'The history of the J-cloth from 1963 to the present time'.
Ursula	Goodness, so you're a sort of academic are you?
Kent	Oh yes. I was all set to be an Oxford don a few months back – it was just a question of me scraping up the bus-fare – but I couldn't see eye to eye with them over the gown. I said Joan Crawford had it right – a padded shoulder demands a platform shoe.
Ursula	I don't really notice clothes – I've had this for years.
Kent	My mother had something similar.
Ursula	Really?
Kent	She used to throw it over her bubble car in the cold weather.
Ursula	This is a lovely old farm table, isn't it? Do you like stripped pine?
Kent	No, I don't. I was brought up in a dresser drawer, so all this brings back the stench of unbearable poverty.
Ursula	Oh goodness! Will you be able to clean it, then, do you think?
Kent	Oh yes. In fact I shall probably get a better finish if I'm shuddering.
Ursula	You see, being a novelist, I get rather engrossed, rather tend to let the housework go …
Kent	Mm, it's the first time I've seen windows so dirty they were soundproof.
Ursula	I've been working so hard, I must sort myself out, change this dress …
Kent	You know that soup down your front?
Ursula	Whoops.
Kent	Well, they don't make it any more. And I wouldn't go swimming till you've washed your hair; it could be another Torrey Canyon.
Ursula	It's just my deadline – my novel …
Kent	There's only one woman novelist struck home with me: Shirley Conran, *Superwoman* – I could not put it down.

Ursula	The new one, *Lace*, have you read that?
Kent	How they could call it explicit! I read right through and I was still no wiser over getting felt-tip off formica.
Ursula	Do you think you'll be able to take this little job?
Kent	Not really, no. I couldn't clean for a woman, I find them a very unnecessary sex.
Ursula	But my name was on the card, it was a woman's name.
Kent	That's no real indication of gender; it could have been an auxiliary fireman dropping a heavy hint.
Ursula	So I can't twist your arm?
Kent	I'd rather you didn't touch anything of mine. I'm very squeamish, skin-wise. In fact my social life took a real up-turn when I found they did Marigold gloves in large sizes.
Ursula	You're a novelist's dream, I could listen to you all afternoon – do stay.
Kent	No, I can't settle. I keep fretting about dysentery.
Ursula	Oh, just a few secs. I mean, where are you from, for instance?
Kent	Well, I was born under a pile of anthracite on the East Lancs Road. My father was a steeple-jack; he got drunk one day and never came down. I left home at fifteen when my mother caught me in bed with a Bleachmatic. I toured the working-men's clubs with a magic act; I used to close with a song. When I got better at it I used to saw myself in half and finish with a duet. Then I went to Monte, modelling ...
Ursula	I'd forgotten all about him.
Kent	Who?
Ursula	Monty Modlyn.
Kent	Monte Carlo, as a model. Got into drugs, marijuana, then cocaine, then Shake 'n' Vac. Then I became a monk, but we had words over my safari jacket.
Ursula	Do you have a close relationship with anyone?
Kent	Well, I've hung round a few lavatories, but I usually only stay long enough to buff up the taps. I'm a loner. There'll never be more than one slice in my toaster.
Ursula	Do you still see your mother?
Kent	Oh yes, I go round once a week, take her some Duraglit or a packet of firelighters. I do have four brothers.
Ursula	What do they do?
Kent	They're a string quartet.

Ursula	So is cleaning your main source of income?
Kent	Well, I won quite a bit of Northumberland in a raffle, so I don't go short.
Ursula	So, you don't really need this job?
Kent	No.
Ursula	What pity! You know, I'd love to put you in a novel.
Kent	Oh, you can put me in a novel.
Ursula	Really?
Kent	Piece of pastry – two pounds an hour, four hours a week, I can squeeze you in between Beryl Bainbridge's seventh, and Melvyn Bragg's twenty-fourth. Just change my name and call me broad-shouldered, all right?

Kitty: Two

Kitty Well, I've come back, as you can see. Kitty. I wasn't struck either way but it was too wet to prick out my seedlings so here I am. Excuse me.

She fiddles with her tongue at a back molar.

The boys in flat five gave me a lattice jam puff to take with and the pips are playing me up. I say pips – I happen to know the jam factory's not quarter of a mile from a firm dealing in balsa wood novelties, so draw your own conclusions.

She gets the pips out.

That's it. They're all my own. In our block, it's always my gnashers they call on if they can't unscrew their dandelion and burdock. One of these fillings is French actually. I went on the hover to Boulogne with the Rummy Club, and we were having a grand time with some pop and a tray of bonfire toffee, when, crack, there I am with bits of molar all down my wind-cheater. I should never have crunched because it was Helen Murchison's toffee, and she doesn't know a soft ball from a dust-pan and brush.

Anyway, consternation all round. In fact Margery Hunt went green, teeth are her *bête noire*, but I think that's because a Swiss dental mechanic once fumbled with her pedal pushers. Now that, for me, would have turned me off Toblerone, but then if we all thought the same, we'd have smaller shopping centres.

So – we land at Boulogne, and I said from the look of those lavatories there won't be a British Consul here, we shall have to ask round. Well, I guessed that the French for dentist would be *donteeste*, knowing how they love to drag a word out, and so it proved.

Helen Murchison reckons to know a bit of the lingo, and she popped me a few words on the back of a *Family Circle* – just the bare essentials: my name's Kitty, could you bung up my hole till I get back to Blighty type thing. I found a lovely man who spoke quite good English, went a bit blank when I mentioned Shepherd's Pie ... he patched me up and said something about money, but I just laughed. That was seven years ago, and I can still crack a Brazil without wincing.

Kitty checks her watch.

It's never twenty to? This has never been the same since it went in the Bournvita. I had my friend Win with me from Kidderminster, and I think we'd had a couple of liqueur chocolates too many.

I don't drink as a rule, not wishing to have a liver the size of a hot-water bottle. If I need a 'buzz', as I call it, I have a piccalilli sandwich with Worcester sauce; that takes your mind off your bunions, believe you me.

I mean, alcohol in excess can cause untold misery, not to mention the bother of humping the empties. A previous lady below me – I shan't name names (do they get this in Cardiff?) – she would come in at a quarter to six, with her carrier bulging, and it wasn't with Arctic Roll, and by eight fifteen she'd be out by the bins, shouting about coloureds. It's never bothered me, race. I don't care if people are navy blue so long as they don't spit up. There was a lot of that in Boulogne, I remember. I said to Marge, they can stick their bread, I couldn't live here.

Well, I can't stop anyway. There's a play on the radio tonight, set in a maisonette, so I shall have my lobes pricked for *faux pas*.

Kitty gets up as before.

Who took charge of my butty-box? Butty! Tuh.

Just an Ordinary School

Film. The school hall: assembly. Girls are singing hymns. One girl, Anthea, is singled out.

Anthea *(Voice Over)*   There are all sorts of girls here, even coloured girls, though they tend to be princesses mainly, but really, on the whole, it's just an ordinary school.

The common room. Babs, Anthea and Ceal are lounging about, chatting. It is all very posh.

Male Interviewer *(Voice Over)*   And do you ever feel guilty about your fathers spending five thousand pounds a term on you?
Anthea   Not really, do you? I don't really.
Babs   My father would only spend it on booze or something.
Ceal   New taps for his yacht or something.
Interviewer *(Voice Over)*   But I mean some parents can't spend that amount of money on their daughters' education.
Anthea   Oh, can't they? No, I suppose no ...
Babs   But you make an effort, don't you?
Ceal   Yes, you find the money, because my cousin's father's a duke, and he's awfully poor actually, and they sold a Gainsborough, quite a hideous one actually, and that sort of brought in enough loot to cover quite a few terms ...
Babs   Anyway, you don't have to have all the extras.
Anthea   Scuba diving – quite a lot of the girls don't do that now, do they?
Ceal   Or ballooning, hot-air ballooning. There's only about ten girls here with their own balloons now.
Interviewer *(Voice Over)*   What I mean is: does it make you work harder, knowing the amount that's been invested in you?

Anthea	No.
Ceal	I mean, a lot of things one learns here, they're not really going to be very much use when one leaves.
Babs	I mean, we're not going to talk Latin, are we?

Laughter.

Anthea Or French!

Laughter.

Ceal	I mean tying my own shoe-laces, I just won't ever have to do that … so why should I spend hours learning it?
Babs	Or cordon bleu.
Anthea	No, I think cordon bleu's quite good, because, if you're in for the evening, right, and you're not being taken out to dinner, and, say, cook's given notice or something, you might need to know how to cook, or you might really get quite hungry … Actually, I cooked chips once.

Babs and Ceal Oh you didn't, what a fib!

Anthea Well, I stood jolly near while somebody else did, so shut up.

They collapse laughing.

The common room. The girls are as before.

Interviewer *(Voice Over)* The feeling in the town seems to be that the pupils here are rather snobbish and stand-offish.

Ceal	People just get the wrong idea.
Babs	Just because one's father's Lord of the Admiralty or something, doesn't mean you're posh, particularly.
Anthea	My father hasn't even got a title. He sent it back, so …
Ceal	People seem to think we sit around eating caviar all day long.
Anthea	When actually we've only had it three times this term.
Babs	And it's jolly cheap caviar anyway.

The dining hall. The girls are queuing up for dinner, holding out thin, white gilt-edged plates.

Anthea   Oh, yuk! *Dauphinoise*, no thanks. What's that?
Dinner Lady *Brochet aux champignons de rosée.*
Anthea   OK, but not too much.
Babs   What is it, Anth?
Anthea   Boring old *brochet aux champignons.*
Babs   Oh, tediosity.

The common room, as before.

Interviewer (*Voice Over*)   What do you think about working-class girls?
Anthea   Well, I think there have to be some, otherwise it would be so hard to get served in shops and things.
Ceal   And for factories, I think factories would close down, actually, if it wasn't for working-class people.
Interviewer (*Voice Over*)   Couldn't you and your friends work in them?
Anthea   We'd be hopeless, honestly. We'd just get sacked, I think.
Interviewer (*Voice Over*)   Babs?
Babs   I can barely fit my bassoon together.
Ceal   Actually, my aunt worked in a factory during the war; it was her factory, and she said a lot of the girls there were really quite decent.
Anthea   On the whole, I think it's better off if we just don't mix, that's why it's so nice here, having the electronic gates, and the moat …

School hall: prize-giving. The orchestra is playing as a girl leaves the stage.

Headmistress   And now the Oswald Mosley prize for public speaking. And the nominations are Elizabeth Finsbury, Nella Parsley-Donne, Chung Lee Suk, and Anthea Fern Witty.

Whoops, having trouble with the envelope, and the winner is – Anthea Fern Witty.

Cheers from the audience. Anthea runs to the front as the orchestra plays a jolly showbiz tune very badly. Anthea and the headmistress kiss, as she takes her prize.

Anthea Oh gosh, I just want to say I'm thrilled to get this ... I'd really like to accept it on behalf of Miss Hewitt and Mrs Winchester. I'd like to thank Babs and Ceal for all the marvellous help they've been to me – and to everybody in the Upper Fifth, I love you – this is for you.

Turkish Bath

Two female attendants, both in bikinis over their everyday clothes, with corporation towels round their heads, are chain-smoking and viewing the proceedings.

Thelm	My God, if her bum was a bungalow she'd never get a mortgage on it.
Pat	She's let it drop.
Thelm	I'll say. Never mind knickers, she needs a safety net.
Pat	She wants to do that Jane Fonda.
Thelm	That what?
Pat	That exercise thing – nemobics.
Thelm	What's that?
Pat	Our next-door does it. We can hear her through the grate. You have to clench those buttocks.
Thelm	Do you? She'll never get hers clenched – take two big lads and a wheelbarrow. Who's she clenching them for, anyway?
Pat	Who, next-door? She's remarried again. He's black with an Austin Maestro.
Thelm	Well, she's got someone to notice then, hasn't she? Our Jack wouldn't. Liberace could come in with a long-line bra but our Jack wouldn't twig on. First night of our honeymoon, I was in bed, he was making a hutch.
Pat	What for?
Thelm	Bugger only knows. Only bloody animal we've got's him. Filthy. I'm taking his vest to the Antiques Road Show. You're separated, aren't you?
Pat	He's living in the loft. He's got the lilo and the slow cooker; we don't speak.
Thelm	That's the blue of our Margaret's shower curtain.
Pat	Where.
Thelm	Them varicose veins, there.
Pat	Nice.
Thelm	Our Margaret's coming off the cap. Says it's dangerous.

Pat	That's the pill.
Thelm	Is it? I better pop her a note through.
Pat	Can you not phone?
Thelm	The doctor says I haven't to dial.
Pat	What's that scar on Mrs Critchley? Appendix?
Thelm	No, it's just where she's nodded off on her Dick Francis. It's very levelling, a Turkish bath, isn't it? Take Lady Templeton, fur coat, Justice of the Peace – to me she's just jodhpur thighs and an inverted nipple.
Pat	Is Miss Hardy all right? – she's very still.
Thelm	She's either passed out or passed on. Either way (*she drags on her fag*) I'm finishing this.
Pat	That's her from the flower shop, isn't it? Her with yellow flip-flops on.
Thelm	Them's her feet, you traycloth.
Pat	Isn't she bony?
Thelm	Well, I'm not rubbing her down. Like trying to massage a xylophone.

There is the sound of a splash , a shriek, a gurgle.

	That's another dropped dead in the cold plunge. Water's too cold. It's getting embarrassing – men coming round to collect their wives and you're saying, sorry she's dead and here's her teeth in a jiffy bag.
Voice	We're ready for a rub down!
Thelm	Hang on! Where's loofah?
Pat	Dog's had it.

Thelm picks up a foul scrubbing brush.

Thelm	This'll do. You bring the Vim.

They amble off.

Kitty: Three

Kitty is caught unawares, sipping her fifth cream sherry, and chatting affably to Morag.

Kitty   No, honestly Morag, I do think that Brillo has helped your freckles. What? Oh, hello. We've been having a running buffet for the last programme. We all mucked in on the nosh; I did my butter-bean whip – it's over there in a bucket. And the director did us a quiche. I suppose it's his acne but I definitely detected a tang of Clearasil.

The producer didn't cook, thank goodness. She's a nice girl, but when someone chain-smokes Capstan Full Strength and wears a coalman's jerkin, you're hardly tempted to sample their dumplings.

Her empty sherry glass is replaced with a full one.

The first day I met her she said, 'I'm a radical feminist lesbian'; I thought, what would the Queen Mum do? So I just smiled and said, 'We shall have fog by tea-time.' She said, 'Are you intimidated by my sexual preferences?' I said, 'No, but I'm not too struck on your donkey-jacket.' Then it was, 'What do you think of Marx?' I said, 'I think their pants have dropped off but you can't fault their broccoli.' She said, 'I'm referring to Karl Marx, who as you know is buried in Highgate Cemetery.' I said, 'Yes I did know, but were you aware that Cheadle Crematorium holds the ashes of Stanley Kershaw, patentor of the Kershaw double gusset, to my mind a bigger boon than communism.' I said, 'Don't tell me the Russian women are happy, down the mines all day without so much as a choice of support hose?'

Her glass is topped up.

It's all right, leave the bottle. In Russia, show the least athletic aptitude and they've got you dangling off the parallel bars with a leotard full of hormones. And what has China ever given the world? Can you really respect a nation that's never taken to cutlery? We bring them over here and what do they do? They litter the High Street with beansprouts. I know what you're going to say – what about the Chinese acrobats?

Kitty is a little inebriated by this stage.

Over-rated. I could hop up on a uni-cycle and balance a wheelbarrow on my eyebrows but I'm far … too … busy. If I was to turn to juggling I should never get any rummy played.

Not that I think Britain's perfect. I see life each week from the train window of my Cheadle Saver, and I think I can safely say, people today aren't pegging enough out.

If I was Prime Minister, and thank goodness I'm not, because I've been the length and breadth of Downing Street and never spotted a decent wool shop. But if I were, I would put a hot drinks machine into the Houses of Parliament and turn it into a leisure centre. The income from that would pay off the National Debt, and meanwhile we could all meet in Madge's extension. I would also put three pence on the price of a flip-top bin, because I don't like them, and use the spare cash to nationalise the lavatory industry, resulting in a standard flush.

I would confer knighthoods on various figures in the entertainment and sporting world, namely David Jacobs, Pat Smythe and Dolly from Emmerdale Farm.

Before I leave you, I must say I've much loved coming here every week to put you right, and I'd just like to pass on a piece of advice given to me by a plumbing acquaintance of my father's. It's an old Didsbury saying, and I've never forgotten it.

Kitty has forgotten it. She sits blankly. No, she can't remember it.

Whither the Arts?

TV studio, arts programme.

Presenter   Later on in 'Whither the Arts?' we'll be visiting the Arnolfini Gallery in Bristol, and taking a look at their Sculpture 84 exhibition, the centre-piece of which is the controversial twenty-foot ironing board made entirely from Driving Test rejection certificates. But first, the much publicised musical *Bessie!*, which opens at last in the West End this week, and Deb Kershaw has been in on the rehearsals, and has sent us this report.

Film. Rehearsal room. People are hanging about. Deb is interviewing the director, the exceedingly pompous fifty-year-old Sir Dave Dixon.

Deb   Could you just tell us a little bit about *Bessie!*, Sir Dave? It's a biographical musical.

Dave   Yes, it tells the story of Bessie, Bessie Bunter, who was an amazing lady …

Deb   Sorry, I thought Bessie Bunter was a fictional character.

Dave   No, Bessie was a real person, very much so, a real person, and she led an incredible life, actually …

Deb   What about Billy Bunter, was he real?

Dave   But oh yes. Though it seems unlikely that he wore those check trousers we – er – see – er – in the illustrations.

Deb   Did you commission the musical, or …?

Dave   I was sent a play about Bessie Bunter, whom I've always been fascinated by, and the very same day I bumped into the American composer, Hamley Marvisch, who said he had a few tunes left over from his last flop, and did I have a show he could dump them in? So two days and a bottle of Scotch later, we'd finished *Bessie!* A day to write the

	show and a day to think of the exclamation mark.
Deb	Has it altered much from the original play?
Dave	We've opened it up a little. The play was very much Bessie Bunter's schooldays, the fat girl with the little round glasses. We've played around with it, we've brought in the Spanish Civil War, the McCarthy witch hunts, that's a nice duet, great dance routine in Sainsbury's with the whole company on shopping trolleys …
Deb	But Bessie's still fat, presumably?
Dave	Well, it's mentioned. We've made it a mental fatness rather than a physical thing. We can't really have a great fat lump walloping across the stage for two hours.
Deb	Is the writer amenable to all these changes?
Dave	Yes, he was fine, most happy …
Deb	Is he here today?
Dave	No, he's had some sort of an accident. I think he fell off Chelsea Bridge with some bricks in his pocket, but we're coping …

Rehearsal room. Thirty-five-year-old serious actress, Carla, stands by pianist in rehearsal clothes. She is very serious, constantly coughing or clearing her throat.

Carla	No, I shan't sing out today, Dennis. I really am going to have to be awfully careful.
Deb	Sorry to interrupt, Carla.
Carla	No, don't worry, Deb.
Deb	Now, you're playing the main rôle, Bessie?
Carla	Bessie, yes – great challenge.
Deb	Is it a difficult rôle?
Carla	Bessie Bunter was actually an incredibly complex person, I've been steeping myself in the literature, and Bessie is so like me, so many similarities, it's quite spooky.
Deb	What have you been reading?
Carla	*Bessie Bunter Goes to the Circus*: now, I went to the circus – that's rather a remarkable coincidence. I've just read *Bessie Bunter Goes Caravanning*: now, I have an aunt who has a caravan, so I've been down and had a look at it. (*Coughs.*) Excuse me, I've got pneumonia.

Deb	Beryl Reid always says she starts with the shoes; if the shoes are right, the character's right. Is that your method?
Carla	I start with the bra. If the bra fits, everything falls into place.
Deb	What's the song you're rehearsing?
Carla	This comes after Bessie has had a secret romance with Anthony Eden, played marvellously by Derek Griffiths, and she knows it's only a matter of time before he goes back to the – was it the Conservative government? Anyway, it should be very effective, I'm wearing beige, and she knows she isn't going to see him again, and musn't see him for his sake – it's called 'One Day'.

She sings.

One day,
a feeling-sorry-that-you've-gone day
I will maybe write a note
send it to float
right to your door.
I won't sign it.
I'll just deliver it and go
and no-one but you will know
who I wrote it for.

One day,
a feeling-slightly-put-upon day.
I will maybe send a rose
that no-one knows
from whom it came.
I won't sign it,
I'll just leave it in the hall,
Maybe blow a kiss that's all,
I won't leave my name.

One day,
a wishing-I'd-become-a-don day
I will maybe try and grab
a London cab
to your bungalow

I won't see you,
I won't even ring the bell,
I will simply wish you well,
then I'll turn and go.

The stage is covered in exhausted dancers. Rows and banging are going on, the piano is covered in eighty-seven coffee cups, Carla is sobbing in the stalls, with pals trying to comfort her. Sir Dave sits in the front stalls, affable and relaxed as before, with Deb.

Deb (*Voice Over*)   The show opens tonight, there have been many changes, the original cast has been fired, and the show drastically rewritten.

Deb   You've gone back to the original concept, Sir Dave?

Dave   This was vital, I feel. I mean, Bessie Bunter is a fat schoolgirl – that's the show in a nutshell. It's about being fat, being at school – it's very exciting.

Deb   So you've cast a fat actress?

Dave   The fatness is crucial. I've been researching into this pretty thoroughly, over breakfast. Do you know that over 89 per cent of people in this country are overweight? Now, that's a lot of tickets. The number we're about to see, if they ever get their (*bleep*) fingers out, is the Act One finale. (*Shouts.*) When you're ready, for Christ's sake, thank you!

The company prepare for the song.

And it's really all about finding yourself, saying take it or leave it, this is me. Because I believe all humans have a value and a right to be respected. *(He turns round to Carla.)* Get the (*bleep*) out of here, Carla, will you? I don't really want snot all over the plush, love. OK Dennis!

'Bessie' walks on-stage dressed as per the Frank Richards books. During the number she rips off her wig, glasses, and gymslip to reveal blonde hair and skin-tight dress. She is backed by a chorus line.

Bessie *(sings)*   One day I was Bessie Bunter.
Who was she?
She was just a punter
She was nobody.

Then suddenly
one hot night
had a brainwave
like a spotlight.
Wave goodbye to Bessie,
say hello to me!

Me!
I'm going to be free
I'm gonna to do all those things I've never done before
open the door!
Let's even the score.
I'm looking for life to go and kick it in the crutch
just a touch
to make it clear
that Bess is here
with her one-woman junta
please watch out for Bessie Bunter.

Me!
who else could it be?
I'm gonna go bleach my hair,
wear clothes that show my tits
at the Ritz
I'm Bessie the Blitz
I'm gonna make Dolly Parton look like Meryl Streep
I mean cheap
I mean bad
drive men mad
to make this girl surrender
will they get to my pudenda?
Don't answer that; dance!

The company dances.

Yes!
Here's looking at Bess!
Here's looking at thirteen stone of sex
who can it be?
well it's me!
come and see
look at me!
you'll agree
it's all me!

At the end of the number she completely drops out of character.

They're going to have to change this floor, I'm sorry ...

Margery and Joan: Three

Joan	And we'll have more needlework hints next week, when Philippa will be showing us how to stitch up the mouth of a talkative friend or relative. And now, as usual on Fridays, we're going over to Margery to see what sort of week she's been having. Hello, Margery, what sort of week have you been having?
Margery	Hello Joan. Well, I've been having a very hectic time. On Monday, my husband and I tiled our bathroom – more on that later – and on Tuesday we filed for divorce.
Joan	And so do you think you might follow the trend, Margery, of the rather worn-out middle-aged woman shacking up with a much younger man?
Margery	Well, it's definitely worth looking into, Joan. One nice thing I do like about younger men is that they tend not to wear pyjamas.
Joan	By pyjamas you mean nightwear generally?
Margery	Yes, and striped garments in particular.
Joan	Yes, because, I know from our postbag, Margery, that many of our viewers find folding pyjamas quite an arduous task.
Margery	That's right, Joan, often leading to lower back pain, depression, dependence on tranquillising drugs, and sadly, alas, to suicide.
Joan	Gosh. But you've also been looking at double glazing, haven't you?
Margery	Cheap double glazing, Joan.
Joan	With the emphasis on the cheap rather than the glazing, Margery?
Margery	Absolutely. So –
Joan	So, in effect, we don't have to spend four or five thousand pounds keeping our homes draught-free.
Margery	No. So –
Joan	So how do we go about it?
Margery	Sorry, could you just move away; your breath smells –

thanks. Right – a new report just out reports that most of the heat-loss lost from rooms is actually escaping through the glass. That's the see-through part of the window. Now double-glazing can cover up the glass, but it can't take it away. Now a new firm has come up with a revolutionary and much cheaper idea of taking the glass away, and bricking up the spaces where the windows used to be. And hey presto, no glass, no draughts, no heat-loss.

Joan   No light.

Margery   No, I suppose not, Joan.

Fade in music, fade out dialogue.

Joan   I suppose you'll prefer to be in the dark, Margery, if you're planning to sleep with lots of younger men?

Margery   Or I may just blindfold them in the lobby, Joan; I'm fairly loose either way.

Madwoman

An oldish, crazy-looking tramp/alcoholic woman is on a bench in the middle of some open concrete area, like a shopping precinct. She's mad and keeps shouting.

Woman   Oi! Who you looking at? Eh? Eh? You wanna get back on your spacecraft you do. Beam me up, beam me up, ha! I can tell spacemen a mile off – oh yes, I've had messages about this.

You look at me here, you think I know nothing – well they seen my brains at Paddington, and they were well pleased, well pleased. Shopping trolley! Tartan, tartan, what sort of pattern's that, eh? Are you Scotch? You don't look bloody Scotch. I been there – Scotch House – I seen their sweaters, very nice wool. They threw me out – I'll be back. Bloody Scotch people, I seen the Loch Ness Monster, and it wasn't talking to Eamonn Andrews, neither.

Oi, trackshoes, trackshoes! Go on, get jogging, fat-arse! Ever had sex? Don't bother. Oh yeah, married twice, oh yeah, telly on, meatballs … Oi! Where's your meatballs, Mister? Ha! We don't need the lot of you, magotty old men, you wanna crawl back under your manholes – just leave us girls the sherry and du-vet. I bet she's got a duvet, old jiggle-tits there. They're coming off, bosoms – it's the Council. (*posh*) Bosoms are off this spring, I hear. Lucky for you, pleated skirt!

Oi! Shirley! Shirley Bassey! You're a bit of a blackie, ain't you? Sorry you saved up now, eh? Ten pounds for a pair of shoes! Huh! I'm off to China, outskirts of China, going down the Left Luggage, little plastic shoulder bag, and I won't write no post-cards.

Don't think I can't, khazi-features! I've had letters from
right round the latitudes and I can lay hands on them, oh
yeah, I can lay any amount of hands on them – no flicking
danger.

What you been buying? Little panties? So's you can go
jigging about your lounge? You won't be laughing when the
Russians put paid to the hot weather. You're laughing now
with your nice little strap shoes and your carrier bags, but
they're on their way – the Russians are coming – they'll
freeze your balalaika for you. Ha! Call yourself a man, Kim
Novak? Filthy habits, the lot of you! Shopping about. Too
much shopping going on. I'm on to the government about
this; oh yeah, I can have this place sealed off – I'm on to it,
I'm not joking, piss-belly! I know a lot of people in that line
– Dave and Bob, heard of them?

And I'll be here tomorrow; I've had messages about this –
this isn't the only planet in the world, jam-lips. (*Points to the
bench.*) Nobody touch that!

She walks away, waving her arms about.

Voice Over   That was a party political broadcast on behalf of the
Conservative Party.

Cast List

Skin Care	*Girl*	Victoria Wood	WW
	Assistant	Julie Walters	
Brontëburgers	*Guide*	Victoria Wood	LB
The Woman with 740 Children	*Woman*	Victoria Wood	WW
	Reporter	Julie Walters	
Young Love	*Gail*	Victoria Wood	VWASOT
	Carl	Andrew Livingston	WW
This Week's Film	*Jean*	Julie Walters	VWASOT
	Smithy	Richard Longden	
In the Office	*Beattie*	Victoria Wood	VWASOT
	Connie	Julie Walters	
Dotty on Women's Lib	*Dotty*	Julie Walters	WW
Cosmetic Surgery	*Girl*	Victoria Wood	VWASOT
	Customer	Celia Imrie	
The Reporter	*Widow*	Victoria Wood	VWASOT
	Reporter	Julie Walters	
	Butch	Jim Broadbent	
On Campus	*Selina*	Tilly Vosburgh	VWASOT
	Mummy	Barbara Graley	
	Daddy	Peter Bland	
	Maggie	Suzanne Sinclair	
	Hilary	Victoria Wood	
Shoe Shop	*Customer*	Victoria Wood	VWASOT
	Assistant	Julie Walters	
	Janine	Celia Imrie	
Dandruff Commercial	*Actress*	Julie Walters	VWASOT
Toddlers	*Toddlers*	Victoria Wood	WW
		Julie Walters	
The Practice Room	*Pianist*	Victoria Wood	WW
	Cleaner	Julie Walters	
Supermarket Checkout	*Till girl*	Victoria Wood	VWASOT
	Customer	Celia Imrie	
Kitty	*Kitty*	Patricia Routledge	VWASOT
This House Believes	*Schoolgirl*	Victoria Wood	LB
Groupies	*Bella*	Victoria Wood	WW
	Enid	Julie Walters	
	Star	Alan Lake	

Margery and Joan	*Joan*	Victoria Wood	VWASOT
	Margery	Julie Walters	
Film Classic	*Barry*	Peter Postlethwaite	VWASOT
	Freda	Kay Adshead	
Service Wash	*Old Bag*	Victoria Wood	VWASOT
The Boutique	*Customer*	Victoria Wood	VWASOT
	Assistant	Julie Walters	
Giving Notes	*Alma*	Julie Walters	VWASOT
Cleaning	*Ursula*	Victoria Wood	VWASOT
	Kent	David Foxxe	
Just an Ordinary School	*Anthea*	Felicity Montague	VWASOT
	Babs	Tracy Childs	
	Ceal	Georgia Allen	
	Dinner Lady	Barbara Miller	
	Headmistress	Zara Nutley	
Turkish Bath	*Pat*	Victoria Wood	VWASOT
	Thelm	Julie Walters	
Whither the Arts?	*Bessie*	Victoria Wood	VWASOT
	Presenter	Duncan Preston	
	Deb Kershaw	Celia Imrie	
	Carla	Deborah Grant	
	Sir Dave Dixon	Patrick Barlow	
	Dennis (pianist)	David Firman	
Madwoman	*Woman*	Julie Walters	VWASOT

LB = *Lucky Bag*, first performed at the King's Head Theatre, Islington, in October 1983.

WW = *Wood and Walters*, shown on Granada TV in January 1982.

VWASOT = *Victoria Wood As Seen on TV*, shown on BBC2 in January 1985.